What to Do When You Are BULLIED for Being DIFFERENT

Addy Ferguson

PowerKiDS press.

New York

Published in 2015 by The Rosen Publishing Group, Inc.
29 East 21st Street, New York, NY 10010

First Edition

Editor: Jennifer Way
Book Design: Erica Clendening and Colleen Bialecki
Book Layout: Andrew Povolny
Photo Research: Katie Stryker

Photo Credits: Cover, p. 1 Dawn Lackner/iStock/Thinkstock; pp. 4, 19, 20 Fuse/Thinkstock; p. 6 ZouZou/Shutterstock.com; p. 7 monkeybusinessimages/iStock/Thinkstock; p. 8 Zurijeta/iStock/Thinkstock; p. 9 wavebreakmedia/iStock/Thinkstock; p. 10 BananaStock/Thinkstock; pp. 11, 22 moodboard/Vetta/Getty Images; p. 12 moodboard/Thinkstock; p. 13 Saintho/iStock/Thinkstock; p. 15 aaron belford/Shutterstock.com; p. 16 Jupiterimages/BananaStock/Thinkstock; p. 17 asiseeit/Vetta/Getty Images; p. 18 Shyamalamuralinath/Shutterstock.com; p. 21 Lisa F. Young/iStock/Thinkstock.

Publisher's Cataloging Data

Ferguson, Addy.
What to do when you are bullied for being different / by Addy Ferguson. — 1st ed.
    p. cm. — (Stand up: bullying prevention)
Includes an index.
ISBN: 978-1-4777-6892-1 (Library Binding)
ISBN: 978-1-4777-6893-8 (Paperback)
ISBN: 978-1-4777-6620-0 (6-pack)
1. Bullying—Juvenile literature. 2. Bullying—Prevention—Juvenile literature. 3. Self-esteem.   I. Title.
BF637.B85 F47 2015
302.34

Manufactured in the United States of America

CPSIA Compliance Information: Batch #WS14PK5: For Further Information contact Rosen Publishing, New York, New York at 1-800-237-9932

Contents

What Is Bullying?

Have you or someone you know ever been bullied? Bullying happens when a person or a group of people pick on, tease, or **taunt** another person repeatedly. When friends tease a friend, they will stop if it starts to hurt their friend's feelings. A bully does not stop when he sees he is bothering someone. He is trying to hurt, scare, or embarrass the other person.

There are many reasons people bully. Bullies often **target** those who are different, though. Kids who have a different weight, color, religion, or who speak a different language from the other kids are often targets of bullying.

For teasing to be OK, everyone involved must be having fun. When it stops being fun for one person, feelings get hurt. If it continues, it is bullying.

Types of Bullying

You may think that all bullying is the same. This is not true, though. There are some bullies who use their words to hurt others. They are called verbal bullies. Physical bullies use their bodies to hurt their victim.

Cyberbullies find ways to reach their targets using computers or smartphones.

Bullying by exclusion means leaving a person out on purpose.

Social bullies convince a group of people to **exclude**, spread **rumors**, or gang up and be mean to a person in other ways. Cyberbullies use technology to bully. They use texts, emails, and social media to bully.

No matter what kind of bullying someone does, it is always wrong. It is wrong to treat others cruelly or unfairly.

Bullied for Being Different

Bullies often choose to pick on people whom they see as different. Their target may dress differently from other kids or like different activities. They may have **mannerisms** that make them stand out as well. These are just a few of the differences that bullies may focus on to taunt their target.

Children who follow a different religion than most of the other kids at school are more likely to be bullied. Bullying someone because of her religion is a form of discrimination.

The kid who gets the best grades might stand out as different and draw the attention of a bully.

Sometimes people are bullied for being part of a **minority** group. Bullies may pick on kids whose skin color is different from their own or kids who come from different cultures. They may also bully people who follow a different religion than they do. Singling kids out for these kinds of differences is called **discrimination**.

Vulnerable to Bullies

Some kids have physical **disabilities** or mental impairments. This includes children who have **autism** or who need to use wheelchairs. Bullies also target kids who are shy or anxious. These kids may prefer to spend time alone or have trouble making friends. All of these differences can make a person vulnerable to being bullied. To be vulnerable means to be more likely to be hurt.

A kid who has a physical disability might need a wheelchair or crutches to get around.

Kids who have mental impairments like Down syndrome are much more likely to experience bullying than other kids.

Bullies are often looking for a way to feel powerful. Picking on people who do not fit in is one way some bullies do this.

How Bullying Affects Kids

Bullying has a lasting impact. Bullying can make kids feel sad, anxious, lonely, scared, and angry. It can also cause them to have low **self-esteem**. Kids who are bullied for being different might dislike the thing that they are being bullied for, like their weight or skin color. This is unfair and makes kids feel very sad.

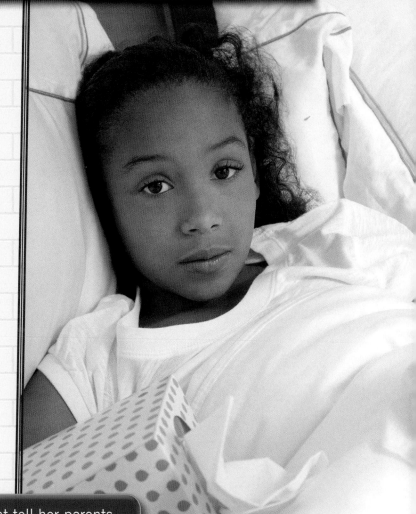

A kid who is being bullied might tell her parents she has a headache or a stomachache so that she can stay home from school and avoid her bully.

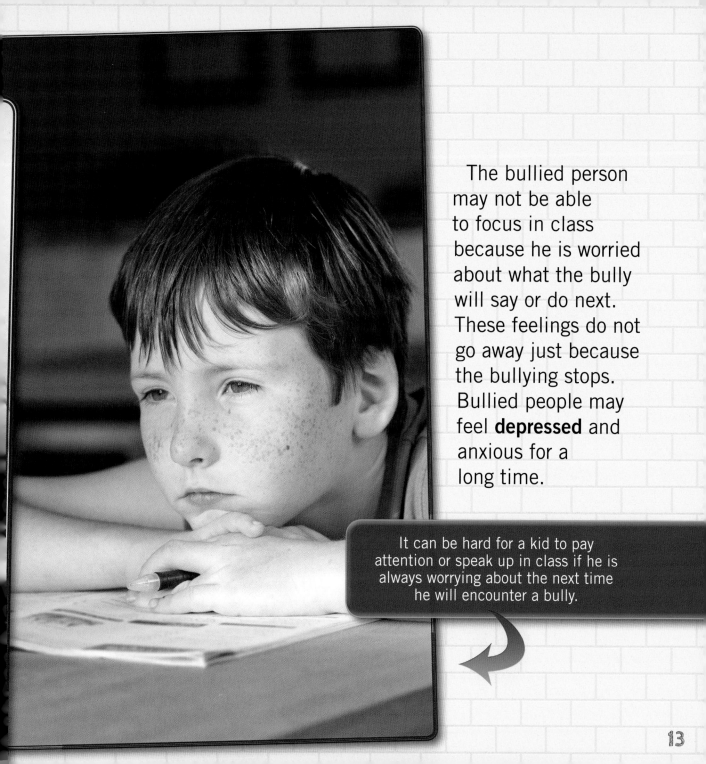

The bullied person may not be able to focus in class because he is worried about what the bully will say or do next. These feelings do not go away just because the bullying stops. Bullied people may feel **depressed** and anxious for a long time.

It can be hard for a kid to pay attention or speak up in class if he is always worrying about the next time he will encounter a bully.

Don't React

Try to remember that bullying is not your fault. One way to deal with a bully is to tell her firmly to leave you alone. You could also just walk away and ignore her. The bully wants a reaction to feel as if she has power over her victim. Walking away or ignoring her denies her that reaction. You may have to do this more than once, but if you keep refusing to react, the bully may give up.

Do not fight a bully with words or your body. This gives the bully the reaction she is looking for and could get you hurt or in trouble.

You could walk to school with a classmate who is being bullied for being different. Sometimes being alone makes a bully more likely to pick on someone.

Talk to Someone

One of the things that helps a bullied person is having someone to talk to. If you or someone you know is being bullied, find a person you trust to talk to. A trusted teacher, parent, coach, or friend can make you feel less alone. A grown-up may also have ideas for making the bully stop.

Talking to a friend or sibling about being bullied is a good first step to getting the help you need.

Talking to a parent or teacher about being bullied is not tattling. Telling a trusted adult is something you need to do to get help with your bullying problem.

You may be worried that telling someone about your problem will only make it worse. Do not think this way. You can even try talking to the bully yourself about the thing he is bullying you for. If you explain your difference to him, he might understand you better.

Making Choices

If you are bullied for being different, you may think that the only way to stop a bully is to change who you are. You do not have to change to stop the bully. Embracing what makes you different from everyone else can give you power. If you feel good about yourself and your choices, it is harder for a bully to target you.

Bullying hurts your self-esteem and brings up a lot of negative feelings. It is important to talk to someone to work through your feelings.

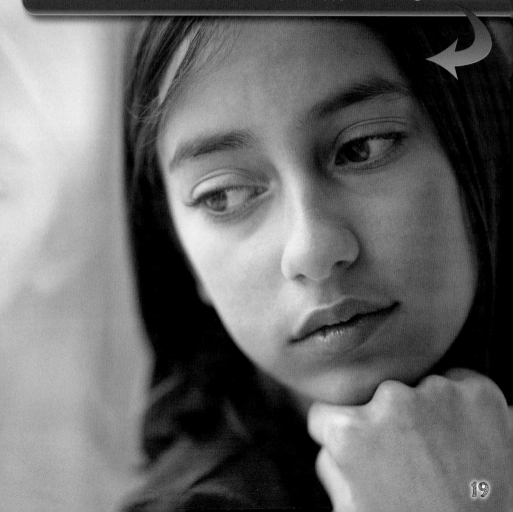

You should change only if you want to, not to please others or to stop a bully. A counselor can help you talk about feelings of low self-esteem related to bullying.

When you are bullied for being different, you might start to doubt the things you like about yourself. Don't change because of a bully. It won't make you happy in the long run.

Zero Tolerance

Many schools are putting zero-tolerance policies into place. This means that bullying will not be allowed to happen there.

Many bullies target kids who are not good at sports in gym class. A school with a zero-tolerance policy watches out for these situations and quickly moves to stop them.

Schools with zero-tolerance policies emphasize that it is important to show respect to every person.

In zero-tolerance schools, the entire community agrees to stand up to stop bullying. Everyone respects one another. Bullying is less of a problem in places where people are supportive and respectful of each other. If your school has a zero-tolerance policy for bullying, you should feel proud. If your school does not have this kind of policy in place yet, you can talk to your principal or a teacher about making one.

Respect for All

No one asks to be bullied. Differences should be respected. Instead of excluding or teasing someone who is different, make a point to get to know that person better. You might learn something interesting and make a new friend.

Even if you are not the one being bullied, you should not stand by while other people are. Use your voice to help stop bullying and create a community where everyone can feel good about himself.

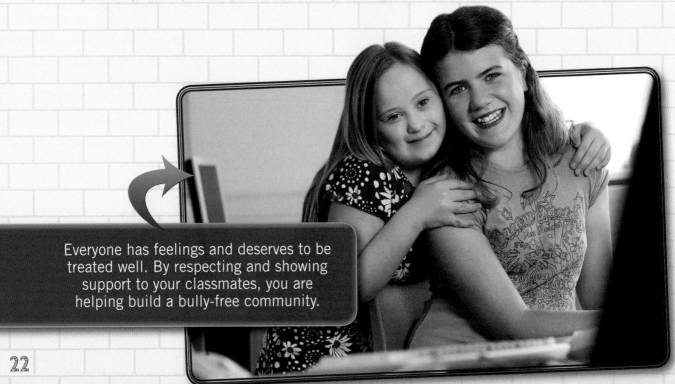

Everyone has feelings and deserves to be treated well. By respecting and showing support to your classmates, you are helping build a bully-free community.

Glossary

autism (AW-tih-zum) A set of problems some people have that may include trouble dealing with others or talking.

depressed (dih-PRESD) Felt very sad for a long time.

disabilities (dih-suh-BIH-luh-teez) Physical or mental conditions that make it harder or impossible for people to do things.

discrimination (dis-krih-muh-NAY-shun) Treating a person badly or unfairly just because he or she is different.

exclude (eks-KLOOD) To keep or shut someone out.

mannerisms (MA-nuh-rih-zumz) People's particular ways of talking, speaking, or moving.

minority (my-NOR-ih-tee) A group of people that is in some way different from the larger part of a population.

rumors (ROO-murz) Stories that are heard by people with no proof that they are true.

self-esteem (SELF-uh-STEEM) Happiness with oneself.

target (TAHR-git) To make someone the object of attention.

taunt (TAWNT) To tease with the purpose of hurting or upsetting someone.

Index

B
bodies, 6, 14

C
color, 5, 9, 12

D
differences, 8–10,
    17, 22

F
feelings, 5, 13, 19

G
group, 5, 7, 9

K
kind(s), 7, 9, 21

R
religion, 5, 9

S
self-esteem,
    12, 19

T
target(s), 5, 8
technology, 7
texts, 7

V
victim, 6, 14

W
weight,
    5, 12
wheelchairs, 10

Websites

Due to the changing nature of Internet links, PowerKids Press has developed an online list of websites related to the subject of this book. This site is updated regularly. Please use this link to access the list: www.powerkidslinks.com/subp/diff/